Medicine Men
Stories of Power

by Pippa Pralen

"Our ancestors had the intuition that there was a secret rhythm in Nature which was the same in every single natural manifestation. A crane dance must mirror star dances, and human dance is an alphabet to decipher the unknown."

Table of Contents

Many early white settlers described powers of the medicine man and women unknown to the Europeans: power to locate game in the wilderness, foresee the future, and heal with herbs and plants.

Mesmerized in Jamestown

In 1609, 400 English settlers arrived in a swampy area of Virginia, establishing a colony called Jamestown. In the first few years most died of starvation and disease. More settlers arrived, and the colony did survive. In 1611, Sir Thomas Dale arrived in Virginia as governor of the Jamestown colony. He decided to explore the country and desired to travel to a waterfall, several days' journey.

Powhatan, Pocahantas and Capt. John Smith

Powhatan the local Indian chief with dominion of 32 tribes, forbade the trip. He also demanded the release of 2 Indian prisoners held by the English. Governor Dale ignored the request and began the journey. Powhatan threatened that if the English journeyed to the falls he "would cripple them with drink" and "make them dumb and then kill them". Dale took the threat as a joke.

The English began their journey. Later, near their encampment, the English heard strange sounds in the forest. Reverend Alexander Whitaker described the noise like "hup hup", followed by "oho oho". Here is his account.

> "a strainge noise was heard comeing out of the Corne towards the trenches of our men, like an Indian hup hup ann Oho Oho, some say that they saw one like an Indian leape over the fire and runne into the corne with the same noyse.
>
> All the while all our men were confusedly amazed. They could speake nothing but Oho Oho, and all generally takeing the wronge endes of their armes ... But (thankes be to God) this alarum lasted not above half a quarter." Whitaker, Rev. Alexander, *Good Newes from Virginia, 1613*.

The English seemed to be in a trance, only able to say two phrases: "hup hup" and "oho oho". They picked up their weapons by the wrong end, unable to use them, and seemed confused and dazed.

Whitaker later reported the incident to authorities in England who concluded it was some type of Indian sorcery. Are there perhaps other explanations? Was it mass hysteria? Were they poisoned with a hallucinogenic root? Or did the medicine man possess a type of power unknown to Europeans?

Ice in July (Plymouth Colony): Thomas Merton of Plymouth and Merry Mount colonies in Massachusetts, reported that a local medicine man, Papasiquineo, made a piece of ice appear in a bowl of water on a hot summer day in front of an English audience. The powwow intoned an incantation, a thick cloud suddenly appeared, a thunderclap was heard, and the ice was seen in the water. Kupperman,

Karen O., *Indians & English, Facing Off in Early America,* 2000.

The Chosen

To the Indian "medicine" means mystery; it is the essential element of his religion. Generations guarded its secrets from the curious and unworthy. This differs from the modern western concept of medicine. The medicine man was a combination of doctor, medium, priest and prophet.

In every Indian tribe, certain men and women were regarded as the possessors of supernatural powers. They were often unique characters. Some had endured severe illness and recovered. They often were solitary figures that spent time alone in the wilderness.

Once recognized and chosen, it was a lengthy and difficult process.

“It took years to learn the chants. They had to learn the songs. They were called chants, and they were long. And then they had to also gather their paraphernalia. They had rattles, they had different kind of wands. Some wore mink collars around. They had different kinds of costumes they put on pieces of clothing.

They had to gather their paints, because they painted a patient's face. ... And it took many years to get to be a medicine man. No, they couldn't just say, "I'm going to be a medicine man,"... because you spend years gathering all this. It's unbelievable, everything that you have to have. It's in some of the books, shows all of the things that the medicine men had with their medicine man kit.” *Northern Arizona University*

They Know Things...

"Now Dad talks of going to a ceremony and ... the medicine men planted the corn in the ground and they actually saw the corn grow and get ears on it. I don't know how they did it. I don't know how. They know things we don't know". (Source: Northern Arizona University)

Tools of Mystery

Tobacco

The native people recognized the power in the tobacco plant. They believed it contained a "spirit". Indians believed that tobacco opens the door between the worlds of earth and spirit.

Tobacco is held as a **sacred plant** by all native American people. The Tucano tribe of South America believe that their ancestors live on a different plane of existence and that tobacco transports them to their ancestors. Tobacco's power can be seen in addiction, in a dangerous way, when it is used without respect.

Eyewitness Tobacco Use:

> Jean de Lery, 1578, described "ritual tobacco blowing" among the Carib Indians. Their chiefs would use a 4-5 foot cane and blow smoke on the men dancing about them, saying "Receive all the spirit of fortitude whereby you may overcome your enemies".

Some Medicine Men drank tobacco juice or smoked tobacco to assist them in entering a light or deep trance, in healing rituals. The light trance leaves the medicine man still conscious and able to commune with his/her guardian spirit without travel. The second, more deep form involves clairvoyance or ecstasy and requires the Medicine Man to lose consciousness where he leaves his body with his guardian. If the patient needs this sort of assistance, it is believed that he or she has lost his soul wherein reclaiming it requires the Medicine Man to retrieve it from the underworld.

Science Confirms Tobacco's Power

Some chemists do confirm that **tobacco produces perceptual changes** in the human brain.

The native ritual tobacco is quite different from the one used in making cigarettes commercially. Tobacco is a member of the nightshade family of plants, which includes potatoes, tomatoes, etc. Almost every tribe in North America grew it. Native Americans believed tobacco was a gift from the Creator.

There are many types of the tobacco plant, and drinking some may be highly poisonous. Tobacco was also used as a medicine by native Americans, to relieve pain, for earaches and other maladies.

John Rolfe of the Jamestown settlement in Virginia, was an early cultivator of tobacco. The tobacco raised in Virginia at that time, *nicotiana rustica,* did not suit European tastes, but Rolfe raised a more popular variety, *nicotiana tabacum,* from seeds brought with him from Bermuda.

It is a curious fact that a high percentage of people suffering with schizophrenia smoke cigarettes to alleviate their symptoms. However, cigarettes may be a poor fix, causing more long-term harm than short-term help.

One hypothesis about nicotine use is that it enhances the focus of the brain and its ability to filter out unwanted external stimuli. Scientists are conducting research in this area. What is especially curious is the way in which schizophrenics and shamans alike seem to use nicotine as an ally.

Both shamans and schizophrenics deal with voices, spirits, and visions.

And while it may be naive to draw too many fast comparisons between shamans and schizophrenics, could the use of tobacco as a control mechanism factor into the research that is being done?

The Drum
To the native, the drum was not a mere musical instrument. Drumming was a shamanic practice, a way to communicate with the spirit world. Armitage, *Religious Ideology Among the Innu of Eastern Quebec and Labrador*

The drum increases Alpha waves in the human brain. In Alpha stage, insights can be received.

Drumming provides the Innu hunter with information on the possible location of game and future success at hunting. As he plays and sings, he falls into a kind of trance wherein he sees "sparks" on the skin of his drum. The size of these sparks, and their location on the drum head, indicate the number of caribou that may be killed and their approximate location in relation to the hunting camp. (Armitage, Peter, *Religious*

Ideology Among the Innu of Eastern Quebec and Labrador, 1992:85)

In explaining how the drum works, the late Francois Bellefleur of La Romaine made an analogy between it and a television. "**It's like a television**. You see all that you are going to kill when you sing with the drum. With the drum, you see the animals you are going to kill. When one is looking for food, one consults the drum, the animals appear on the surface of the drum." Armitage, Peter, 1992.

Traditionally drumming was a privilege reserved for the elder Algonquins, for men who had dreamed of it, three times.

"The ability of drumming to induce trance states has been scientifically confirmed. Experiments during the 1960's revealed that repetitive sound patterns (sonic driving), such as drumming or rattling, at a certain frequency can induce altered states of consciousness (i.e., an SSC).

Rattling alone can contribute to a trance-induction, but most often rattling accompanies drumming. Ceremonial assistants learn a particular drumming rhythm in order to facilitate a shaman's trance-induction. If the assistants 'misbeat' the drum, the shaman just becomes normal right away (i.e., comes out of the trance). The simplicity of this technique is what makes drumming the preferred trance-induction technique among shamans worldwide. Singing and dancing often accompany the drumming to facilitate the trance-induction.

Not everyone uses drums. The Takelma and Klamath of southern Oregon, and the Wishram of southern Washington, had no drums. Instead, they rested one end of a notched stick on the ground and rasped it with another stick. The point here is that we are dealing with sound rhythms. Even the South America ceremonies that use psychotropic plant mixtures to induce the SSC are filled with some form of 'sonic driving.' We are dealing with processes that involve rhythms, what physicists call waves." Lyon, William S. PhD. *Spirit Talkers: North American Indian Medicine Powers.*

Telepathy

The telepathic abilities of medicine men were well known to the early settlers. When a child wandered off into the forest and was missing, and searches were unsuccessful, the parents would often consult with the medicine man, who invariably located the child.

Account of Cecil Denny (Canadian Mounties)

The following account is from Cecil Denny a member of the Canadian Mounted Police in the 1870s:

"These Medicine Men had to my own knowledge great powers of their own, and some of the feats they accomplished were to the least, extraordinary, and those which came under my own observation, I could in no wise account for.

I have seen a Medicine Man, when the camp had been without meat for a long time, and the Indians had no knowledge of where the buffalo were to be found, leave the camp, and go alone to the summit of some hill in the vicinity. There he would remain sometimes as long as three days, without either food or water, making what he called medicine and communing with the Great Buffalo Spirit for power to lead a herd of buffalo into the starving camp.

Medicine woman, No-ah-tah, 1913

He would plaster himself from head to foot with a white clay and burn certain herbs in his pipe, after which he would return to the camp and announce that the Spirit had been propitious and that on the following day he would go out to the plains and draw a herd of buffalo after him to the camp, and for the Indians to be prepared for the slaughter.

I have myself seen this Indian leave camp one day dressed in either a buffalo robe with the horns on, or else with a huge wolf skin round him, **and return after a day's absence with a large herd of buffalo not far behind him**, and this, when no buffalo had been known to be anywhere in the vicinity".

Reading the Bones

Hunters resorted to bone divination or "scapulimancy" in times of extreme need. It was a powerful ritual and not performed in a casual manner. They had absolute faith in the ritual. It is not to be confused with "fortune telling". Divination has ancient roots. Modern children play "cat's cradle" with strings, unaware its original use may have been related to divination.

"Divination is a search for the trend of the divine will, hidden beneath the surface chaos of aspects and events: and God's will can be detected, but not to manipulated". Maria Silva Codesca, *"Of Knots and Dots and Coconuts: Divination in Micronesia".*

The following are types of divination practiced by native American medicine men and women:

Scapulimancy is a type of decision procedure used by natives whereby a bone such as an animal's shoulder bone, is held over hot coals or thrown into fires, causing cracks in the bone which are then analyzed and used to direct a hunting party.

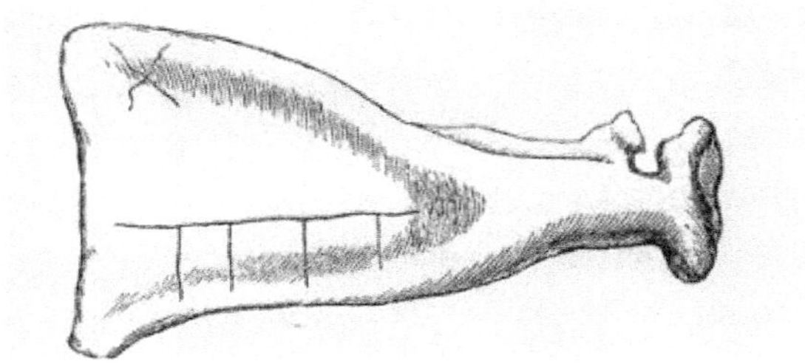

Examples: A porcupine or elk or caribou scapula is held in the fire until it is charred and cracked. The scorch marks and cracks are then studied like a map, to determine the possible location of game.

Innu Bone reading ritual:

"When burning the shoulder blade, they hold the narrow portion of the bone toward the body, the wide portion away from the body, and then as the burnt spots and cracks appear these indicate the directions and locations to be followed and sought." ~ Frank Speck, anthropologist

How does it work?

The tribe needs to locate the caribou herd on the vast tundra. If they are unsuccessful, they will starve. They cast the bone into the fire and the medicine man examines it carefully and tells the tribe to pack up their belongings. They will move to where the medicine man says the herd is traveling.

The Shoulder-Blade Path

The Naskapi are an Algonquin speaking people who live in northern portions of Quebec-Labrador regions. They practiced caribou divination only in winter, when food was scarce.

Sociologist Omar Khayyam Moore observed in 1957, the question divination answers: "*What direction should hunters take in locating game?*"

Anthropologist's theories of Effectiveness:

Overrides Fixed Patterns:
Scapulimancy works because it suggests to the hunter a "random" place to hunt for game, one that might not necessarily have occurred to the hunter otherwise. It provides an advantage in avoiding a fixed or habitual pattern in hunting. There is often a tendency for hunters to return to sites where previous hunts may have been successful.

It is theorized that the cracks on the bones act as tools to override the cluttered rational thought and access the deeper intuitive thought, which may have more validity.

Avoids Overhunting:
Animals that are "overhunted" are likely to become sensitized to familiar patterns of hunting and would be quick to take evasive action. "Reading the bones" introduces irregularity, or the element of surprise, into the hunting patterns and avoids depletion of game.

Anthropologists tell tales of great hunger among the Innu tribe. The location of the herd of caribou was unknown to the tribe. The medicine man was given the task of 'divining' the exact location in the wide expanse of wilderness. The anthropologist was skeptical and scared he might perish from hunger with the tribe.

The Medicine Man threw the shoulder bone of a caribou into a fire. He took the burned bone out and slowly read the black marks of the burn lines. The anthropologist thought "My God we are going to starve".

The tribe traveled in the direction advised by the medicine man, although it was very far. Lo and behold a large caribou herd was at the exact spot. The tribe survived. The anthropologist was convinced.

While shamans would foretell the future hunting success for a whole band of hunters, great emphasis was also placed on each individual's personal ability to obtain religious power, through dreams, through songs and by following the correct rituals and feasts, which were held in conjunction with hunting activities. *The Newfoundland and Labrador Heritage Website*

Divination was utilized by ancient Europeans. "The divination by *taghairm* was once a noted superstition amongst the Gael and in the northern parts of the Lowlands. When any important question concerning the future arose, some shrewder person than his neighbor was pitched upon, to play the part of prophet. This person was wrapped in the warm smoking hide of a newly slain ox or cow, commonly an ox, and laid at full length in the wildest recess of some lonely waterfall. The question was then put to him, and the oracle was left in solitude to consider it.

Here he lay for some hours with the cloak of knowledge around him, and over his head, no doubt to see the better into futurity; deafened by the incessant roaring of the torrent; every sense assailed; his body steaming; his fancy in a ferment; and whatever notion had found its way into his mind from so many sources of prophecy, it was firmly believed to have been communicated by invisible beings who were supposed to haunt such solitudes". Alberfeldy, A., *Radical Linguistics*

Divining Battle Strategy
Divination was used to predict battle strategy before going on the war path.

John Tanner, the Ottawa white captive, provides a description of this ritual. Objects were psychically moved by the medicine man in a cleared piece of ground. Enemy plans were revealed as well as what course the war party needed to follow.

Tanner: " in their encampments at night, the chief who conducts the party, sends some of his young men ... to prepare what is called '*Pushkwaw gnmnie genahgun*', the piece of cleared ground where the ... divination by which the position of the enemy is to be discovered... is to be performed. The chief ... goes and sits down at the end opposite that of the enemy's country; then, after singing and praying, he places before him, on the margin of the piece of ground, ...two small roundish stones.

After the chief has remained here by himself for some time, entreatin the Great Spirit to show him the path in which he ought to lead his young men, a crier goes to him from the camp, and then returning part way, he calls by name some of the principal men saying, ' come smoke.'

.. then examine, by striking a light, the result. The two stones ... have moved across to the opposite end, and it is from the appearance of the path they have left in passing over the soft ground, that they infer the course they are to pursue." (narrative John Tanner)

John describes other mysterious events in his narrative. John Tanner forgot how to speak English, and fully adapted into native culture. He became a great hunter. In 1817, when he was 22, he left his native family and began the trip to reach his birth family.

Upon his arrival, many tears were shed as his brothers, sisters, and neighbors gathered around. John needed a translator to communicate in the English tongue. He eventually returned to his Indian family in the North, and worked as guide and interpreter at fur trading posts. He recounted many mysteries he witnessed in the narrative of his life.

White Captives

It was not uncommon for pioneers living at the age of "civilization" to be taken captive by native tribes. Some returned with tales of strange and extraordinary powers of the native medicine men and women, powers unknown to European or "white" culture.

John Tanner

In 1790 John Tanner lived with his homesteading family near the Kentucky frontier. When he was nine years old, two Ojibwa men grabbed him as he played one spring day near his father's cornfield.

They took John captive, taking him deep into the northern wilderness of the Great Lakes. He was adopted and lived as an Indian. John witnessed mysterious practices of medicine men and women unknown to the Europeans. These were later recorded in a narrative of his life.

The following is an account of how John Tanner's adopted mother, Netnokwa, psychically located game and food when they were close to starvation.

"With the deep snow and thick ice, came poverty and hunger. We were no longer able to take beaver in traps, or by the ordinary methods, or kill moose. "

The old woman spent a night in prayer and singing.

"In the morning, she said, 'Go and hunt, for the Great Spirit has given me some meat.' But... the weather was too cold and calm, and no moose could be approached so near as to shoot him.

'I can make a wind'
answered Netnokwa

'and though it is now still and cold, the warm wind shall come before night. Go, my sons ... in my dream I saw you coming into the lodge with a beaver and a large load of meat on your back'. The hunters left in a desperate search for game.

"They had not been a long time absent, when the wind rose from the south, and soon blew high, the weather, at the same time, becoming warmer.

At night, they returned, loaded with the flesh of a fat moose ... as the old woman had seen him in her dream." Tanner John, Edwin, James, *Narrative of the Captivity and Adventures of John Tanner,* Cargill 1830.

Scoouwa

James Smith was born in 1737, in Franklin county, Pennsylvania, at that time the backwoods frontier, the extreme limit of civilization.

In May 1755, at the age of eighteen, James was working on the Braddock Road, in central Pennsylvania. He was taken captive by the Delaware Indians, adopted into an Indian family, and accompanied them in all their wanderings, untilIt his escape in 1759.

Soon after he was taken, he was forced to run the gauntlet and later underwent an adoption ritual. The Indians named him "Scoouwa".

James Smith runs the gauntlet

Adoption - Becoming an Indian

He was led to a river by Indian women, where he feared they would drown him. However, the women stripped him of his clothes and pulled out his hair, washing him ceremoniously.

He went through a whole day-long ritual, where by in the end, the chief gave a moving speech indicating that all the white blood had been washed out of this man's veins.

James, like many captives, describes the unusual powers of the medicine man. He describes "bone reading" by a medicine man, which seemed prophetic:

One day at a maple sugar camp, a squaw raised an alarm. She thought she had seen two men with guns in their hands, upon the bank on the other side of the creek., which were believed to be Mohawk Indians.

"Before we withdrew from the tents they had carried Manetohcoa (the medicine man) to the fire, and gave him his conjuring tools; which were dyed feathers, the bone of the shoulder blade of the wild cat, tobacco, &c v and while we were in the bushes, Manetohcoa was in a tent at the fire, conjuring away to the utmost of his ability.

At length, he called aloud for us all to come in, which was quickly obeyed. When we came in, he told us that after he had gone through the whole of his ceremony, and expected to see a number of Mohawks on the flat bone when it was warmed at the fire, the pictures of two wolves only appeared. He said though there were no Mohawks about, we must not be angry with the squaw for giving a false alarm ... so he said we might all go to sleep, for there was no danger and accordingly we did.

The next morning, we went to the place, and found wolf tracks, and where they had scratched with their feet like dogs; but there was no sign of mockason tracks...I am persuaded that the Indians believed what he told them upon this occasion, as well as if it had come from an infallible oracle; or they would not, after such an alarm as this, go all to sleep in an unconcerned manner. If there is any such thing as a wizzard, I think Manetohcoa was as likely to be one as any man". Bradford, John, 1799, *An account of the remarkable occurrences in the life and travels of Colonel James Smith*

Great Spirit's Providence

Smith (Scoouwa) tells of being stranded in the wilderness with an old Mohawk man and his grandson during a drought. They were 40 miles from any other humans. They were hungry and without food. Natives used the rivers as highways to travel to find game, but the water level was low in the river and they could not use their canoe to travel and were desperate.

James thought their plight was hopeless.

The old man searched for some fox and wildcat bones the dogs had discarded on the ground and made a broth to strengthen

James. James was the only able-bodied man to hunt for the old man and boy.

The old Indian told James he would begin to fast and pray to the Great Spirit for help, especially for rain, so James could travel to hunt. James laughed at the absurdity of it all, but the old man chastised him, saying he did not laugh at his beliefs, and James should show some respect. The old man spoke to James:

"*Brother, As you have lived* with the white people, you have not had the same advantage of knowing that the great being above feeds his people, and gives them their meat in due season, as we Indians have ..I know that you are now afraid that we will all perish with hunger, but you have no just reason to fear this. Brother, Owaneeyo (Great Spirit) some times suffers us to be in want, in order to teach us our dependence upon him.

Be assured that you will be supplied with food, and ... the great spirit will direct your way." *Scoouwa, James Smith's Indian captivity narrative. James Smith,* William McCullough Darlington. Ohio Historical Society, 1978

The old man chanted and prayed to the Great Spirit for 2 days. When he finished **the rain began to fall in torrents.**

James Smith recounts his desperate search for game: As the water level rose, James was able to search for game and hunt.

"It was now that I concluded I would run off to Pennsylvania, my native country.... I then proceeded on as fast as I could walk, and when I got about ten or twelve miles from our hut I came upon fresh buffalo tracks...I ran with all my might and headed them, where I lay in ambush, and killed a very large cow. I immediately kindled a fire and began to roast meat, but could not wait till it was done; I ate it almost raw...

When hunger was abated I began to be tenderly concerned for my old Indian brother and the little boy I had left in a perishing condition. I made haste and packed up what meat I could carry, secured what I left from the wolves, and returned homewards".

I scarcely thought on the old man's speech while I was almost distracted with hunger, but on my return was much affected with it ... I also considered how remarkably the old man's speech had been verified in our providentially obtaining a supply."

James later admitted that he was amazed at these events. *Could the prayers of the old man have affected nature and the weather?*

In 1760 James Smith returned home to live with the "whites" or settlers:

"Early in the year 1760 I came home to Conococheague, and found that my people could never ascertain whether I was killed or taken until my return. They received me with great joy, but were surprised to see me so much like an Indian, both in my gait and gesture"

He eventually re-adjusted to the non-Indian world. His extensive knowledge of Indian customs and warfare proved a valuable asset during the colonial wars.

The Shaking Tent

The earliest record we have of the "shaking tent" is from the explorer Samuel Champlain. In 1609, Champlain spent time with the Algonquin warriors. While Champlain wanted the warriors to keep watch at night, they refused. Instead, they conducted a shaking tent ceremony and consulted the spirits about the nearness of any enemies. The spirits indicated that no enemy were near and so the warriors slept. Biggar, 1925, Vol2: 86

It was a serious ritual, involving some danger. The shaking tent, or "conjuring lodge," was the setting for a powerful divinatory rite. The shaking tent could foretell events, obtain knowledge of enemy movements, gain information about people who were not present, find causes and cures for diseases. Vecsey, Christopher, *Traditional Ojibwa Religion and Its Historical Changes, Volume 152*

It was performed by specially trained shamans across much of the Great Lakes and Subarctic regions. The "tent" was a small booth built of saplings. The medicine man entered it and a vortex of powerful energy often filled the tent, according to witnesses, where strange voices were heard, and unusual sights seen as the tent bent and trembled with power.

In the western U.S., some native Americans described seeing future visions of the white settlers during a Shaking Tent ceremony – they were amazed at the different color clothing, having never seen white people, nor heard their strange language. This was in the early 1600's long before the first settlers migrated.

The lodge would shake from the power emitted.

After the shaman entered the frame, it was completely covered with bark or cloth. Onlookers could hear strange sounds issuing from inside as the tent swayed wildly from side to side.

During his transcendent state, the shaman could dispatch a supernatural helper, usually a mystical turtle, to distant regions to answer questions from his audience about the most auspicious places to hunt, the well-being of distant relatives, and what would happen in the future.

"The shaking tent would tell you exactly where the animals being hunted are. For example, if you wanted to kill caribou, it would tell you exactly where the caribou are. It's as clear as we are talking to each other now." Tipatshimuna Collections, Virtual Museum of Canada, Mani-Matinen (Gregoire) Nuna, September 23 1993

Witness:
When talking about the shaking tent in English or French, younger Innu borrow technological vocabulary from Euro-Canadian society to describe it. For example, one Innu youth from La Romaine said the shaking tent "was as powerful as an atomic bomb", that "there "was a kind of electricity in the air when it operated", and "the shaman could communicate with people 'telepathically' while in the tent". Armitage, Peter, *Religious Ideology Among The Innu Of Eastern Quebec And Labrador*

Native people said about the shaking tent, "it's very similar to a radio... If there were people far away... and you wanted to communicate with them, then you could do the shaking tent." Armitage, Peter. *1982. Field notes, research at La Romaine, Quebec* Tipatshimuna Collections, Virtual Museum of Canada

"People often remark they can hear the spirits coming to the ceremony as they hit and penetrate the skin or blanket covering. The spirit lodge noises often reach a crescendo and sometimes appear to be several different voices. At this point in the ritual, the medicine man asks the questions that people have posed and receives answers from the spirits. The people often addressed the spirits or "manitous", asking questions and seeking advice. At times exchange is witty and ribald.

The stream of levity misled some white observers to consider the rite unimportant.

After the questions have been answered, the tent becomes stable again, and the medicine man emerges, totally exhausted. Some tribes... have the medicine man enter completely naked and carrying a pipe." Deloria Jr., Vine, *World We Used to Live In: Remembering the Powers of the Medicine Men*

In a major study of the Innu shaking tent, Sylvie Vincent notes that the medicine man communicates with the animal masters but only with the assistance of his *Mishtapeu,* a giant spirit being who comes from the other world. Sylvie Vincent, «Structure du rituel: la tente tremblante et le concept de *mistapew*», in *Recherches amérindiennes au Québec*, vol. 3 1973.

"Stout poles and timbers, immovable otherwise, demonstrate great flexibility during the ceremony and are stiff and inflexible before and after the ceremony takes place. ... people have to admit that the voices are different and that they engage in conversation with some voices appearing to be speaking from the top of the tent, while others are definitely heard at ground level." *Vincent, Sylvie*

Like a Radio

"Certain members of the Montagnais habitually repair to the woods, set up a log shelter about the size of a telephone booth, get inside and, when the power is sufficiently strong, make contact with a friend or relative who may be hundreds of miles away. A two-way conversation is carried on seemingly by clairaudience. If no contact is made, it is assumed that the person with whom contact is sought has died." (Vine Deloria : *The World We Used to Live in : Remembering the Powers of the Medicine Men.* Fulcrum Publishing, 2006.)

Shaking Tent Account of Cecil Denny, Canadian Mounted Police (1870s):

"Another instance I well remember, which I was fortunate enough to see, was to say the least, peculiar, and I confess startled me not a little.

I happened to be camped in the summer of 1879 on the Red Deer River, and in close proximity to a large Blackfoot Indian camp. One moonlight night I walked over to the camp with my interpreter, intending to visit the lodge of the medicine man, which was pitched on one side, and a little way from the main camp.

We entered the lodge which had only a small fire burning in the centre. The medicine man was sitting wrapped in his buffalo-robe at the head of the lodge, and smoking one of their long medicine-pipes.

He paid no attention to us whatever. I therefore sat down next him, placing a present of two plugs of tobacco beside him, and lighting my own pipe, proceeded to quietly smoke without a sign of recognition being made by the Indian. Everything was very still in the lodge, while outside in the main camp, drums could be heard beating in different parts where dances were being held. We had sat quietly this way for some little while, when I was suddenly startled by the sound of a bell ringing above me over the top of the lodge. I could see nothing, and the Indian made no move.

Presently the tent itself began to rock, even lifting off the ground a foot or more behind me. When it is remembered that a large Indian tent consists of dozens of long poles crossed at the top, and wide apart at the bottom, and covered with buffalo-hides, it will be seen that it is nearly impossible to lift one side, and no wind can blow them over.

The rocking motion ceased after a while, and I went outside the lodge to see if anyone had been playing tricks, but not a human being was in sight near us.

The moon was very clear and you could see a long distance. On my returning and resuming my seat, after a short time the tent again began to rock, and so violently this time that it would sometimes be lifted several feet on one side, so high that you could plainly see outside.

My interpreter was thoroughly frightened, and I was not much better, but the Indian never made a single move. We had seen enough however, and left the lodge, returning home to our camp completely mystified. The trick, or whatever it was, certainly went beyond me". Denny, Cecil, *National Archives of Canada*, RG-18, vol. 3437, officer's file 25, 1909.

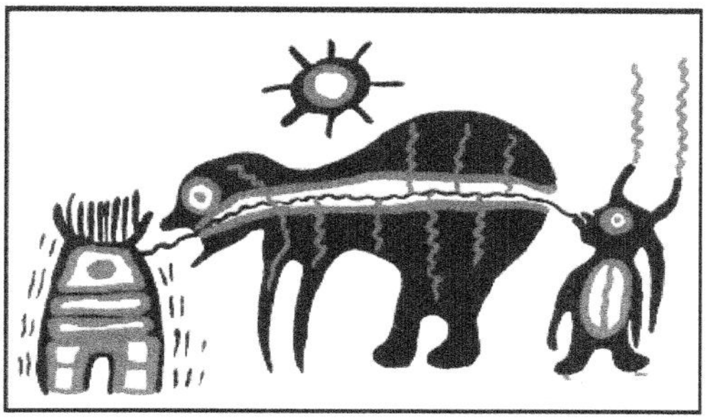

It is said these ceremonies are still being performed in the wilderness areas of Canada.

Wamponoag Religious Practices

The Indians who greeted the Pilgrims of Plymouth Colony in Massachusetts were the Wamponoag. The medicine man of the Wamponoag were as a “pawwaw”.

Hobbamock was a local pawwaw or medicine man who came to live with the Pilgrims. He was considered so powerful, that if he entered a battle field, the Indians would flee immediately.

The tribes of New England were eventually virtually wiped out. Those that weren’t wiped out were confined and no longer the powers they had once been.” A devastating war erupted “King Philip’s War”, led by the son of the Chief Massasoit, the friend of the Pilgrims.

There had once been a great friendship between two peoples – the Pilgrims at Plymouth and the Wampanoags, a very strong relationship for at least 15 or 16 years. Two distinct and different cultures met, and both were changed forever.

Unusual Feats

Medicine men often performed astounding feats.

Falling Geese

"A missionary among the Crees, Edgerton R. Young, told me of a white man who was once out hunting. He came upon an old medicine man, who begged him for game, as he was hungry. The white man made sport of him, saying, 'You are a great medicine man; why not get game for yourself?'

The old man was enraged. He cried out, 'White man, see yonder goose,' and pointed his finger into the air. The goose fell fluttering at their feet, and the old man picked it up and walked away". Starr, Frederick, *American Indians*, 1898

A Dead Otter Walks

Here is an unusual account of medicine men in Alabama. A dead otter is made to walk:

"they work sorceries, like causing to walk the skin of an otter, dead for more than two years, and full of straw. They work many other sorceries which would appear incredible to the reader. This is why I do not want to stop here. I would not even mention it if I, as well as many other Frenchmen who were present there with me, had not been witness of it. Those who perform such feats, whether they are magical or otherwise, are very much esteemed by the other savages. They have much confidence in their prescriptions for diseases".

Swanton, John R., *Early History of the Creek Indians and Their Neighbors*

Finding Lost Items

Many settlers resorted to the medicine man to find a lost child that had wandered away into the wilderness.

Lost Horse

Here is a description of a man who sought a lost horse and saddle:

"Once they got the [yuwipi man] from Slim Buttes...The saddle was a long way off I guess. They had about 20 singers and every other man had a drum. You could hear the saddle coming. They lit up the lamp and told him to see if it was his. He examined it and it was his...

The next day he wanted his horse back so they sang a lot of songs. They sang all night that time. They said, 'you will go up a valley and see many birds. And under the birds you will find your horse'.

He went up that hill and there was his horse and it was dead, shot, and all kinds of birds over it. Ha! It was there and but it was dead and they never would tell who done it". Thomas H. Lewis. *The Medicine Men: Oglala Sioux Ceremony and Healing (Studies in the Anthropology of North American Indians)*, 1992.

Mountain Sheep Struck Lifeless

That the doings of the Kootenay shamans made considerable impression upon the missionaries may readily be believed from the statement attributed to a Jesuit missionary in 1861: "I have seen many
exhibitions of power which my philosophy cannot explain. I have
known predictions of events far in the future to be literally fulfilled,
and have seen medicine-men tested in the most conclusive ways.

I once saw a Kootenia Indian ...command a mountain sheep to fall dead, and the animal, then leaping among the rocks of the mountain-side, fell instantly lifeless. This I saw with my own eyes,
and I ate of the animal afterwards. It was unwounded, healthy, and
perfectly wild. Ah, Mary save us ! the medicine-men have power
from Sathanas." Chamberlain, Alexander F., *Kootenay Medicine-Men*, The Journal of American Folkore, April 1, 1901

Levitation

"James Beckwourth, the famous scout who became a war chief under the name of *Medicine Calf* among the Crows, has related to a friend an extraordinary feat of levitation which a great war chief of the Crow Indians performed in his presence on the eve of leading his warriors to battle.

The chief was an aged man and professed to have a premonition of death. For many moons he had led the Crows successfully against their hereditary foes, the Blackfeet.... his medicine had lost its potency. In the dusk of the gray morning he led his braves out on an open prairie, and, setting his shield on edge some fifteen or twenty feet in front of them, pointed to it with his lance.

As the eyes of the fighting men rested upon the embossed surface of the buckler it appeared to rise slowly from the ground until it reached a height corresponding to the head of the chief; it then, by the same invisible means, passed through the air until it obscured his face and hid it from his warriors.

A thrill of horror pervaded the assemblage, but no word was spoken. It was taken as an emblem of his approaching eclipse, his banishment from this world, his journey to the land of the Great Spirit, to which all Indians, good and bad alike, went with unhesitating faith.

The great chief was killed that morning." Kellar, H., *Magic Among the Red Men*, The North American Review, Nov. 1, 1893

Belt Becomes Rattlesnake

In 1916 in Rapid City there was a celebration. Several medicine men attended. One of the medicine men "Chases the Spiders" stepped forward and removed his belt. He tied his sacred medicine stone to it, rubbed it with sage, and placed it gently upon the earth. In less than a moment he turned into a rattlesnake, which began to crawl away.

The crowd screamed and drew back. Whereupon “Chases the Spiders” retrieved it. The snake turned back into a belt. Mails, Thomas E., *Fools Crow,* Univ. of Nebraska Press, 1979.

Birds Descend from the Sky
In the 1950s in Flagstaff Arizona during an Indian celebration, the medicine man Fools Crow performed an unusual feat.

A small tree was in the center of the arena. Fools Crow sat near the tree and prayed. Suddenly little white birds that shone like white lights swarmed above in the sky and then swooped down from the sky, settling upon the tree. The tree lit up like a Christmas tree. When asked how he performed this feat, he said, he just prayed to Wakan-Tanka to allow him to enjoy his powers in this moment. Mails, Thomas E., 162

Shapeshifting
Man-to-Animal, Animal-to-Man
Modern man recognizes the link between beings in terms of molecular biology and DNA.
There is a recognition that everything is of the same "building materials", the same 103 basic atoms. Only the combinations and architecture vary.

Most native peoples believed in **communication between beings of different species,** or "non-human beings. In this group of not-human beings we find the " hearts " of the major animals (caribou, bear, beaver, bobcat etc.).

Techniques (or channels) of communication are the dreams, the divination (by means of burned bones, drums, etc.), the ceremony of the trembling tent, or the " gazing " (or concentration using usual objects). Speck, F.G. *Naskapi: The Savage Hunters of the Labrador Peninsula, Univ. of Oklahoma Press, 1977*

Note: Anthropologist and ethnographer Frank Gouldsmith Speck, unlike other ethnographers of his time who focused their studies on the western Indian tribes of America, chose to study the cultures of the Eastern Woodland Indians. Becoming the self-appointed ethnographer for those tribes, Speck was regularly with the Indians he studied, collecting all aspects of their culture.

Innu Hunter in Caribou coat

Obtaining Power

For the Innu, men obtain *manitushiun* or hunting power through their hunting activities. It accumulates with age only as a result of maintaining good relations with the animal masters.

The more one hunts, the more *manitushiun* one is able to accumulate. To reach that high degree of psychic power requires much practice, courage, and perseverance. Dangers and terrors must be faced, dangers of a psychic nature, the creation probably of one's own psychic exercise or perception.

Powerful shamans, although old, were still good hunters who had shown throughout their lifetimes that they were able to keep good lines of communication open with the animal masters.

Power also comes from time alone in the wilderness or forest. The Vision Quest is a ritual that connects to that power.

Indigenous people, especially medicine men/women spent much time with their own thoughts, reflecting on dreams, and being ready, at any moment, to enter a condition of receptivity. The quietness and silence of so much of their life, the absence of rush and of urgent appointments, and the fewness of their numbers facilitate this occupation with the psychic. Moreover, their totemistic and animistic view of life predisposes them to it.

The various psychic powers attributed to them must not be too readily dismissed as mere primitive magic, for many of them have specialized in the working of the human mind and in the influence of mind on body and of mind on mind. These are not idle words, for the true doctor-men impart a sense of power and confidence.

The psychiatrist Dr. J.E. Cawte wrote, as a result of a field study... "If faith and hope are healing emotions, the *punmun* [medicine man] mobilises them as do psychotherapists in other cultures" and does so by using "elements common to all psychotherapeutic systems" together with scientific knowledge available in his culture. A.P. Elkin, *Aboriginal Men of High Degree* 1977, 1994.

Dakota Ceremony

Wesley R. Hurt, Jr. and James H. Howard

The Dakota *Yuwipi* rite is a variant of the "shaking tent" ceremony. The rite involves the "calling of spirits" by supernatural means and usually features the shaman demonstrating his prowess and contact with the mystic powers by freeing himself of tightly tied bonds.

Among the Dakota the conjuring ritual is performed for curing illness and the finding of lost and stolen items.

The *Yuwipi* ceremony is always held in a dark place, i.e. a dwelling with all the windows and cracks covered. Formerly a tipi was commonly used. No wires, ropes, or cords are permitted except those to be used in the ceremony. Rawhide ropes are preferred for binding the shaman. Several hundred bags of tobacco are strung together, going around the inside of the house in front of the spectators, who are seated next to the wall. The men sit cross-legged on the floor; the position of the women is not important.

The four assistants then begin to sing, accompanying themselves with hand drums. The songs used are called wakan olowan (spirit songs) and are known to only a few individuals.

Leonard Eagle, a youth of Mandan-Hidatsa and White descent, described attending a ceremony with a group of young men who were quite skeptical. When the gourds began flying about the room one paused, rattling loudly, before one of Eagle's companions. The companion asked him, "Should I hit it?" whereupon he struck the gourd with his fist. The gourd flew to the other side of the room, only to return and strike the youth several times around the face. "It really raised hell with him!" commented Eagle. Wesley R. Hurt, Jr. and James H. Howard, *Southwestern Journal of Anthropology* Vol. 8, No. 3 (Autumn, 1952), pp. 286-296

The Sweat Lodge

Sweating or using a sweat lodge was a common spiritual practice among native indigenous people of North America.

In the early 1600s, a Dutchman named David de Vries in the New Netherlands colony (which would later be New York) wrote an account of a Mahican sweat bath (collected in Jameson's *Narratives of New Netherland*).

“When they wish to clean themselves of their foulness, they go in the autumn, when it begins to grow cold, to make, away off, a small oven, large enough for three or four men to lie in it. In making it they first take twigs of trees, and then cover them with clay, so that smoke cannot escape. This being done, they take a parcel of stones, which they heat in a fire, and then put in the oven, and when they think it is sufficiently hot, take the stones out again and go and lie in it, men and women, boys and girls, and come out perspiring, that every hair has a drop of sweat on it. In this state they plunge into the cold water; saying that it is healthy, but I let its healthfulness pass; they then become entirely clean, and are more attractive than before."

Account of William Penn

William Penn, the founder of Pennsylvania, wrote down a description of how his Lenape friend, Tenoughan, made use of a sweat lodge in the winter of 1683 to cure himself of a fever. Penn wrote in his journal:

"I found him ill of a fever, his Head and Limbs much affected with Pain, and at the same time his Wife preparing a Bagnio for him: 'The Bagnio resembled a large Oven, into which he crept, by a door at the one side, while she put several red hot Stones in a small Door on the other side thereof, and then fastened the Doors as closely from the Air as she could. Now while he was sweating in this Bagnio, his wife was, with an Ax, cutting her husband a passage into the River in order to the immersing himself, after he should come out of his Bath.

In less than half an Hour, he was in so great a Sweat that when he came out, he was as wet as if he had come out of a River, and the Reak of Steam of his body so thick, that it was hard to discern any bodie's Face that stood near him. In this condition, stark naked (his Breech-Clout only excepted) he ran to the river, which was about twenty Paces, and duck'd himself twice or thrice therein, and so return'd (passing only through his Bagnio to mitigate the immediate stroak of the Cold} to his own house, perhaps twenty paces further, and wrapping himself in his woolen mantle, lay down at his length near a long (but gentile) Fire in the midst of his wigwam, or House, turning himself several times, till he was dry, and then he rose, and fell to getting us our Dinner, seeming to be as easie, and well in Health, as at any other time."

Jesuit Relations:
We find a considerable amount of even earlier information regarding sweat lodges in the Jesuit Relations, the yearly reports sent by Jesuit missionaries in 'New France' (the present-day Canadian province of Quebec) to their superior in France... in the Jesuit Relations for the Abenaki Nation of Vermont, LeJune's Relation (1637). the priest observed:

"Here is something quite remarkable: towards evening of the 26th, they prepared a sweat, which was followed by a feast I never saw anything like it in my life: 20 men entered, and almost packed themselves upon one another.

Even the sick man dragged himself thither, although with considerable difficulty, and was one of the troop, he also sang for quite a long time, and in the midst of the heat of this sweat he asked for water with which to refresh himself, -- a part of which he drank and the rest he threw over his body. An excellent remedy, forsooth, for a sick man on the verge of death!

So the next day I found him in a fine condition..."

Lenape Indians

David Zeisberger, the Moravian missionary who lived among the Lenapes in the 18th century wrote:

"It is a custom of the Indians, even when they are tired or have caught cold, to go into a sweating oven several times a week. ... every town has on its outskirts a sweating oven. It is built of timber and boards, covered completely with earth. They crawl in through, a small opening, the latter being closed as soon as they have gone in. A fire is usually built in front of the opening before they go in and hot stones placed in the middle of the enclosed area.

Not long after they have entered, they are covered with perspiration, then they crawl out and cool off, returning to repeat the same thing three or four times. Women have their own sweating ovens though they do not use them as commonly as do the men."

Divining the Future

In the Relation of Hierosme Lalemant [a Jesuit missionary] for 1646, a description is given of a medicine man's use of the sweat house to divine the future:

"On another occasion, before setting out for war, a medicine man was consulted. A bark sweat house 3 or 4 feet high and wide was built for him and inside were placed hot stones. The medicine man shut himself inside the sweat house and sang while the warriors danced outside. Finally, his spirit gave him the answer and he yelled out, 'Victory! I see the enemies coming toward us from the south. I see them take to flight I see all of you making prisoners of them.' On the basis of this, the warriors departed for the south."

Healing

Medicine men used water to heal. Early settlers and missionaries described the "spitting" of water employed by medicine men, often in derogatory terms. The following is an explanation from the Indian's point of view.

Water Healing

"Water seems to hold an important place in the practice of ... Medicine The songs say: 'Water was sent into the wound, water will be sent to his wound,' etc.

It is said the buffaloes heal their wounds with their own saliva, and there are Indians who declare that they have actually seen a wounded buffalo being doctored by others of the herd, who would lick the wound, and blow through their nostrils what seemed to be saliva." La Flesche, Francis, *The Omaha Buffalo Medicine-Men, An Account of Their Method of Practice,* 1890, Journal of American Folklore

Medicine men save a fatally injured boy

La Flesche describes an incident where a young boy was shot in the head and had a life-threatening wound. A group of native Medicine Men rushed to attend to the boy for the entire night, chanting incantations, rattling and using water mixed with herbs, which they spit upon the suffering boy.

“After the doctor had started the song, he put the bits of root into his mouth, grinding them with his teeth, and, taking a mouthful of water, he slowly approached the boy, bellowing and pawing the earth, after the manner of an angry buffalo at bay. All eyes were upon him with an admiring gaze.

When within a few feet of the boy's head, he paused for a moment, drew a long breath, and with a whizzing noise forced the water from his mouth into the wound. The boy spread out his hands, and winced as though he was again hit by a ball. The man uttered a series of short exclamations, "He! he! he!" to give an additional charm to the medicine.”

The “white” agent/physician travelled to the look at the boy, declaring that he might soon die from the fatal wound. The family of the wounded boy refused the offer to visit the white doctors.

The medicine men continued to treat the boy. Within a month he was recovered and returned to playing with his companions.

Stella McGee Tanner: born 1906, Kirtland, New Mexico. Source: Northern Arizona University. Stella describes how a medicine man cured her very sick baby.

"...He never seen a well day (her baby). We had to feed him with an eye dropper for the first two weeks when he was born, because he couldn't nurse or anything, and when he'd cry, he sounded just like a little mouse.

Chunk (her husband) was telling this medicine man about his little sick baby. And so one morning after he'd told him that, we heard a loud noise out in front of the store and the blatting of... a goat. Chunk went and opened the door for him, and it was this old medicine man stood there.

He had this milk goat, and he said to him, 'Now, you give your baby this milk from this goat, and he'll get well', because he had diarrhea so bad he couldn't hold anything down.

And from that day on, then he started to gettin' better. So I've always thought an awful lot of the medicine man, because I feel like he saved my oldest son's life with that". *Northern Arizona University.*

We Talked with the Animals

Many medicine men recounted a time in the past, when medicine men communicated with the animals. This communication allowed the animals to instruct man in man things, in medicine and survival.

It was described as an ordinary event. What this exactly means is not completely clear but suggests a deep and subtle connection.

The following is a description of a strong relation between a medicine man and the bear family. It tells of strange bear behavior upon his death.

An old Chief died in Alaska in the 1970's. His family was a member of the Bear clan. "As his body was taken back to be buried in Angoon,

as the truck rolled by,
bears materialized out of the woods
and lined the road.
Some of the bears stood up".

Martin Calvin L., *The Way of the Human Being,* Yale University Press, 1999

“At other times, when too many bears came out of the forest some of the elders would talk to the bears, telling them they might scare the children, and to stay away. Bears respected this.” *Calvin L. Martin*

> *Note:* Calvin L. Martin was a former professor of history at Rutgers University. Martin spent a summer on a Navajo reservation and lived for two years with Yupik Eskimos in southwestern Alaska. He has written explorations of Native American ways of being and seeing.

Removing a Chiinde

“... I was threatened by a Navajo, and he told me in Navajo--he got very angry at me over something, I don't know. And he come in and he'd been drinking, and he was a big, tall man. In Navajo he says, 'I'm gonna kill you."

I told him, 'Well, go ahead, help yourself.' And he was mad at me, and things kept goin' kinda haywire. I had a flat tire on my truck, and this and that.
The boy I showed you that worked for me for thirty years there, he said, 'I think they put the ***chiinde*** on you and hexed you.' So we had a guy come in and do a sing right in the store. I had to buy a blanket, and I think I paid him $125.
He come in and done this sing. He had some crystals. Then he started his sing and chant...
Anyway, when he got done singing, he held this crystal up. You've seen 'em, I don't know where they are, but it's a Navajo crystal, about that size.

Held it up, and there was a horse and a man on a horse, and a man leading a horse.

And I couldn't hardly tell, and he told me who it was, Perry Ness. He said, "Can you see it?" He held it around and I looked, and then I recognized him. And he said, "That's the one that's giving you the problem."

After we had that sing, I had no more problem with that family or that group of people. Now, you can laugh if you want to, say, 'That's a fairy tale!' but my family saw it, I saw it, and I swear to God it was on there--a guy leading a horse, and a man on the horse; the same man [that had threatened me] " *(source: Northern Arizona University).*

Hungry Times – Finding Game

"After we had remained about three months in this place, game began to be scarce and we all suffered from hunger.

The chief man of our band was called *'the Little Assinneboin'* and he now proposed to us all to move, as the country where we were was exhausted. Our necessities became extreme. My mother talked much of all our misfortunes and losses, as well as of the urgent distress under which we were then laboring.

At the usual hour I went to sleep, but **I was wakened by the loud praying and singing of the old woman**, who continued her devotions through great part of the night. Very early on the following morning she called us all to get up, and put on our moccasins and be ready to move.

She then called Wa-me-gonabiew (her son), and said to him, in rather a low voice, "My son, last night I sung and prayed to the Great Spirit, and when I slept, there came to me one like a man, and said to me,

> **'Net-no-kwa, tomorrow you shall eat a bear**. There is, at a distance from the path you are to travel to-morrow, and in such a direction, ...a small

round meadow, with something like a path leading from it; in that path there is a bear.'

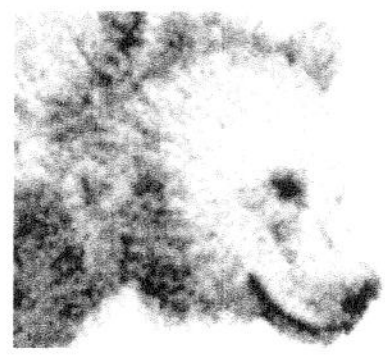

'Now, my son, I wish you to go to that place, without mentioning to any one what I have said, and you will certainly find the bear, as I have described to you."

But the young man, who was not particularly dutiful, or apt to regard what his mother said, going out of the lodge, spoke sneeringly to the other Indians of the dream. 'The old woman, tells me we are to eat a bear to-day; but I do not know who is to kill it.'

At length, I resolved to go in search of the place she had spoken of, and without mentioning to any one my design, I loaded my gun as for a bear and set off on our backtrack.

At length, I found what appeared at some former time to have been a pond. It was a small, round, open place in the woods, now grown up with grass and some small bushes. This I thought must be the meadow my mother had spoken of; and examining it around, I came to an open place in the bushes, where, it is probable, a small brook ran from the meadow; but the snow was now so deep that I could see nothing of it.

My mother had mentioned that when she saw the bear in her dream she had, at the same time, seen a smoke rising from the ground.

I was confident this was the place she had indicated, and I watched long, expecting to see the smoke; but wearied at length with waiting, I walked a few paces into the open place, resembling a path, when I unexpectedly fell up to my middle into the snow. I extricated myself without difficulty, and walked on; but remembering that I had heard the Indians speak of killing bears in their holes, it occurred to me that it might be a bear's hole into which I had fallen, and looking down into it, I saw the head of a bear lying close to the bottom of the hole. I placed the muzzle and discharged it.

As soon as the smoke cleared away, I endeavoured to lift him out of the hole; but being unable to do this, I returned home, following the track I had made in coming out. I went into my mother's lodge.

...I stepped up to her and whispered in her ear, 'My mother, I have killed a bear.' 'What do you say, my son?' said she. 'I have killed a bear.' 'Are you sure you have killed him?' 'Yes.' 'Is he quite dead?' 'Yes.'

She watched my face for a moment, and then caught me in her arms, hugging and kissing me with great earnestness, and for a long time. The bear was sent for, and, as being the first I had killed, was cooked all together, and the hunters of the whole band invited to feast with us, according to the custom of the Indians." Tanner J., Edwin, J. *Narrative of the Captivity and Adventures of John Tanner,* Cargill 1830.

Invisibility

The word 'Apache' often struck fear into people's hearts, and for good reason. The Apache Indians were formidable enemies. The US army was continually frustrated, as they were elusive, and impossible to capture. They seemed to move almost "invisibly" in their familiar terrain.

Artist: Bev Doolittle

A primary reason why so many Indians were employed as scouts by the U.S. government was their talents in observation and tracking. The Apache knew that physical fitness from an early age was necessary for survival.

"Prepared from infancy, the warrior was a master of stealth, cunning, alertness, and fighting skills. He was a superb specimen of physical strength and endurance, running miles without tiring and foregoing food and water for long periods of time." ~ historian Robert Utley

Training of Apache warriors included advanced techniques of camouflage and invisibility as well as of observation and stalking. These skills led to their nicknames as "shadow people" and "ghosts". The scouts became masters of wilderness survival.

This was necessary, for they often had to leave the clan for extended periods of time with nothing but a buckskin loincloth and perhaps a stone knife.

The scouts were taught a highly complex system of tracking, utilizing miniature topographic features within each footprint. These features could tell the trackers anything from the speed at which the quarry was moving, to the direction the quarry was looking. Some tracking experts, such as Tom Brown, Jr., assert that scouts could know whether the quarry was hungry, pregnant, or had to urinate, and to what degree.

Invisibility:
Many ancient cultures had secret invisibility knowledge. Some people describe cloaks or clouds, which is speculated to be related to light absorbing energy. People also talk of curving light. It's deep knowledge and I have no deep grasp of it yet, and will continue to research. Here are some descriptions of Apaches:

“They could lie on the ground and by ingeniously making use of materials near at hand, earth, grass, bushes, etc., could, chameleon-like, appear the exact color of their environments. They would haunt the road and lie in ambush for a day or more to attack a wagon train, which they knew was en route”. Humfreville, James. Lee , *Twenty years among our hostile Indians, 1903*.

“Another excellent illustration of their skill in concealment was given me by Nah-kah-yen. We were hunting together, when a large herd of antelopes made its appearance. Nah-kah-yen immediately tore off a small strip from an old red handkerchief and tied it to the point of a yucca stalk, at the same time ...he instantly buried himself under the sand and grass with the ease and address of a mole.

I at once moved away several hundred yards, and sought to creep up to the antelopes, who were evidently attracted by the piece of red rag fluttering on the yucca stalk. ... In a little while a marked commotion was noticeable in the herd, which galloped off very rapidly for a hundred yards or so, but soon recovered their equanimity, and again approached the attractive red rag. These strange agitations occurred several times, until the antelopes finally dashed away over the plains with wonderful speed. Nah-kah-yen then arose and beckoned me to come, which I did, and found that he had killed four of the herd. We had all the meat our horses could well pack, but the distance to camp was only five miles and soon made." John Carey Cremony, *Life Among the Apaches*

Basics of camouflage:
Silent, slow movement, avoiding hills, don't create a shadow, blend with the shadows, take advantage of light.

Wide Angle Vision
"All animals and primitive hunters and gatherers use this type of vision.

Animals can sense when you tunnel in on them. If you adopt the Native American way of looking, which is called "wide-angle vision", you will become more aware, and see more wildlife. Instead of focusing sharply, look toward the horizon and take in everything directly ahead and to the sides at once, as if you were looking through a wide-angle camera lens. Wide-angle vision will allow you to pick up the slightest little movement.

Wide-angle vision is the doorway to invisibility. It can make you more spiritually sensitive, and will carry you out of the land of the living dead and into the land of the spirit that moves through all things". Tom Brown, Tom Brown Tracker School/

Geronimo, Medicine Man

Geronimo was a renowned medicine man. Historically, his talent as a guerilla fighter eclipsed his other role, especially to non-natives. But among his own people he was an esteemed medicine man.

Geronimo was a Chiricahua Apache, born in Mexico. His given name was *Goyahkla,* (The One Who Yawns), but as a young man he earned the moniker "Geronimo". Geronimo's "white name" may be a result of his fearless and resourcefulness as a warrior. While leading a charge against Mexicans, according to legend, the Mexicans began to shout 'Geronimo!' seeking help from their patron saint, Jerome, or Geronimo in Spanish. To this day, the name remains a battle cry.

In 1850 when Geronimo was on a trading expedition, his mother, wife and three children were murdered by Mexican soldiers. This event affected Geronimo and he was determined to exact revenge on Mexican and American soldiers.

Geronimo, Medicine Man

It is very important to remember that Geronimo was not only a guerilla fighter, but was also a medicine man.

As a medicine man, we must assume he had powers. He was well known among his people as having extra-sensory powers, powers of prophecy, to control movement of clouds, to control the environment and other powers. Here is an eyewitness account from an Apache warrior:

Controlling Time

"When he was on the warpath, Geronimo fixed it so that morning wouldn't come too soon. He did it by singing.

Once we were going to a certain place, and Geronimo didn't want it to become light before he reached it. He saw the enemy while they were in a level place, and he didn't want them to spy on us. He wanted morning to break after we had climbed over a mountain, so that the enemy couldn't see us. So Geronimo sang, and the night remained for two or three hours longer I saw this myself. It seems that these powers select for themselves". Terrell, *Apache Chronicle*

Those who followed Geronimo credited him with a variety of supernatural powers including the ability to heal the sick, slow time, avoid bullets, bring on rainstorms and even witness events over great distances. They believed Geronimo could see the future and walk without creating footprints.

Seer

In one incident described by Apache Jason Betzinez, a few warriors were sitting around a campfire during a raiding expedition when Geronimo suddenly had a premonition that U.S. troops had attacked their base camp. After arriving at the site several days later, they found that Geronimo's vision had been correct—the Americans had already captured the encampment. "I cannot explain it to this day," Betzinez later wrote, "but I was there and I saw it." Evan Andrews, History.com.

Power of Observation

As hunters, many native Americans had by necessity developed keen observation skills. They observed animals and their ability to camouflage.

The fox and the coyote were recognized and observed as elusive animals gifted in evading capture.

As a night creature, foxes are usually seen at dawn and dusk. Dusk starts off their day, and the dawn is its ending. I have often seen foxes at night, and they usually see me before I see them, and am merely given a quick view of a bushy tail entering the dark the forest.
Foxes live on the edges of forests and open lands, the border areas. There are various species of fox, but they all share the extreme cleverness and cunning that paved the way for the expression, "sly as a fox." They are agile, skilled, and unpredictable.

Fox's power lies in not being able to outrun the hounds, but to know in advance when they will be out hunting. They then use their ability to camouflage. A fox being followed by hounds will run across the tops of walls, cross streams diagonally, double back on its trail, run in circles – in short, do anything to break the trail of its scent. Fox has the amazing ability to outwit both predators and prey, how to slip out of unpleasant situations quietly and unnoticed.

Tricky as they were, Apaches would build false camps to confuse the enemy and drive their livestock several miles ahead of the actual area where a group concealed themselves. Camps could be moved silently and were at times moved right under the noses of the Apache enemies. Fight or flight, the Apaches were very skilled in doubling back like a fox and ambushing their pursuers.

Many Apaches described the power of Geronimo as that of the coyote. The coyote was known as a "trickster", an unpredictable spirit, with great cunning.

Geronimo with General Crook

"After Geronimo mourned the death of his family in the traditional way of cutting his hair short (a symbol of mourning) and burning those personal belongings of the people who are dead, he is said to have ventured off into the desert. There alone in the starkness of his desert surrounding he held his head in his hands and wept bitterly. Suddenly a audible voice spoke to him saying "***No gun will ever kill you. I will stop the bullets of the Mexicans and guide your arrows.***"

Geronimo later said he had been given what the Apache people call "Power".

According to "many waters" Geronimo had "Ndaa K'ehgodih" – a prayer power that worked on the midst of his enemies to make their bullets miss their intended targets and turn into water.

The Apache elders say he had this power living inside him and it helped him survive on the battlefield, and allowed him to commune directly with spirits of the animals of the desert. Soon after this "voice" spoke to him Geronimo put this power into action. He asked for and got permission to exact revenge on the Mexican soldiers who killed his family.

With a force of some 200 men he lured the Mexican soldiers into battle. With Geronimo leading the way in a hurl of bullets he is said to have weaved and dodged the bullets killing with his knife the soldiers he came into contact with, when the arrows ran out.

Seeing him run in zig zag patterns and yelling like a man possessed by "diablo" the Mexican soldiers were scared to death, many ran are said to have dropped their weapons and ran away. They had never seen a guy like this before – they nicknamed him the 'devourer of men'. It cemented his reputation in that part of the world." *Robert Tilford*

> *"Power is everywhere. It lives in everything. It might be known through a word or come in the shape of an animal. We all have power but some tap into different rooms. Power speaks to those who listen. The greatest thing a person can have in Apache belief is power!"*
> ~Apache Medicine Man 1889

For 25 years Geronimo and his band eluded the US federal authorities.

On May 17, 1885, Geronimo and some 135 Apache men, women and children took flight from their reservation. The famed warrior was then in his 60s, but he remained as determined as ever, often pushing his group to cover as much as 70 miles per day to avoid the American cavalry and Apache scouts on their trail. Over the next several months, Geronimo's fugitives raided countless Mexican and American and settlement, killing several civilians. They nearly surrendered in March 1886, but Geronimo and 40 followers reneged on the agreement at the last minute and escaped under cover darkness.

Soon, the Indians were being pursued by 5,000 U.S. soldiers—nearly a quarter of the standing army—as well as some 3,000 Mexicans. Geronimo was able elude both forces for over five months, but he and his followers had grown weary of life on the run. On September 4, 1886, he finally gave himself up to General Nelson Miles at Skeleton Canyon, Arizona. In laying down his arms, he became the last Indian leader to formally surrender to the United States military.

Using Plants
The Harvard ethno-botanist, Mark Plotkin, in his book, *"Tales of a Shaman's Apprentice: An Ethnobotanist Searches for New Medicines in the Amazon Rain Forest"*, said he observed the medicine man who accompanied him in the jungle, prescribing plants for earache and other diseases and finally asked him, 'How do you know the uses of the plant? How do you know which plant is good for what ailment?'

The medicine man looked at the botanist like he was stark raving mad. He answered, "Why, the plants tell us, of course". Dr. Plotkin later discovered that this plant communication occurred during trance states and other altered perceptual states.

Plants are life itself. Our breath, our food. Plants are alchemists of life force –breaking it down to be usable for humans. Giving us oxygen and consuming our breath, carbon dioxide. We are already in strong communion with plants.

When to gather plants:
There are times when the plant properties are inert, and times when the medicinal ingredients are at their best, as, for instance, just before the plant blooms, or when the sap is first moving. Paying attention to phases of the moon is important. The Indian has learned to recognize these periods in his own way and proceeds accordingly.

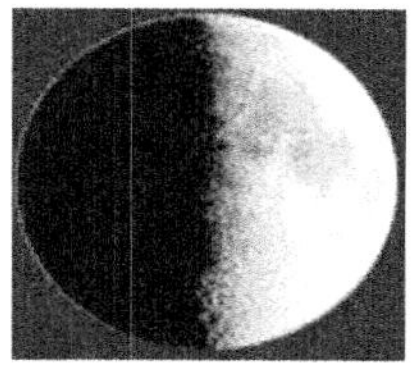

Plants were taken with respect, prayers and sacred chants were given, permission was asked. Some medicine men and women placed a small portion of tobacco in the hole left by the roots of the plant they took.

Plant Communication - Wizard of the Amazon

A fascinating true story about plant communication can be found in the books "*Kidnapped in the Amazon Jungle*", and "*Wizard of the Upper Amazon*" by Manual Cordovo-Rios. Rios was a Portuguese cook working with a rubber company in the heart of the remote Amazon in 1907. He was kidnapped by an Amazon Indian tribe. He was brought into their culture and took sacred plants such as Ayahuasca.
During these sessions, the men entered a "dream state", and he recounts how the plants "would speak to them, advising of their medicinal uses". This is very foreign to western cultures.

The "Huni Kui", the tribe with whom Manuel lived, firmly believed the chants used with the plants were an integral part of the power.

Manuel-Rios underwent a complete shamanic initiation and become a well-known healer.

North American native medicine men felt that reverence of the sacredness of plants is crucial. Reverence imbues the plant or plant medicine with the loving energy which is very powerful. It is holy.

Many herbalists suggest that to access the plant wisdom, you must spend time with the plants to gain intuitive knowledge. One method is to select a plant "to work with" for a year or more and meditate near it, absorbing its ways, observing its environs, how it interacts, watch it sway in the breeze, "live with it".

A State of Wellness
With plants as medicine, the healer acts as an "intermediary" between the sacred power of the plant and the sick person. But many indigenous healers aim for something more than "disease curing". A state of "wellness" is described as "harmony between the mind, body and spirit." It is subtler and deeper than a simple absence of disease. The Cherokee word "*tohi*" meaning 'health' - is the same as the word for peace.

The Cherokee medicine man or *tsila* learns not only the subtleties of every day spoken Cherokee, but a separate "medicine language". Training to become a traditional Cherokee healer takes 15-20 years as an apprentice to well established medicine man.

In order to gain the power to heal a *tsila* must master seven areas of knowledge: herbal medicine, physical medicine, dream work, language/myths/laws, ceremonies, the laws of nature, and conjuring. To master herbal medicine, a Cherokee healer must know the medical and ceremonial use of approximately 400-600 species of plants. Equally important is to master how the plants interact with other substances. David Winston 2001.

Conjuring:
There really is no word in English that fully describes 'conjuring'. Various words – conjuring, magic, manipulation – partially explain this practice. This is the ability to enlist the aid of spirits and elemental powers to change things, to heal or doctor, to "change one's mind", to bring luck, and to protect the sick or weak from negative influences. (David Winston, herbalist)

Subtle Connection:
The Cherokees say they received their plant knowledge from the plants themselves. "It is still a common practice among Cherokee herbalists to walk through the woods allowing the needed medicine to announce itself by unusual shaking or other obvious signs" (Winston). This ability is a true and deep connection, perhaps lacking in the modern era.

Ceremonial Preparation: The dozens of plants used for physical or spiritual well-being by Oklahoma Seminoles today are considered useless without appropriate ceremonial preparation. This includes, in many cases, infusing the plant material in water, singing a prayer, and "bubbling" the infusion by blowing into it through a reed or cane pipe. Some say that the bubbling causes the song or prayer to enter the medicine. Some say that the way the air bubbles through the medicine predicts how well it will work.

The False Face Society

The False Face Society is probably the best known of the medicinal societies among the Iroquois Indians, especially for its dramatic wooden masks. The masks are used in healing rituals. Those cured by the society become members. Also, anyone who dreams that they should be a member of the society may join. The myth or story of the False Face Society is rich. Here it is:

“The Creator having just completed forming the earth, was walking around admiring his handiwork when he noticed what appeared to be another man in the distance, walking toward him. The Creator asked the stranger where he had come from. The stranger replied, ‘I believe that I am the creator of this land, and I am walking around now admiring what I have done’"

Surprised, *Shogway adihs ooh* (the Creator) said, ‘No, you are wrong. It was I who created this land’.

They bickered back and forth like this for a little while, until finally the Creator said, "Fine then, let us have a test to see who actually did create this land." He pointed to a mountain in the distance. "See that mountain?" he said. "We will use our power to move it. The one who moves it the farthest must have the most power, and must therefore also be the creator of this land." The stranger agreed to this challenge, and added his own rule: "We will turn our backs," he said, "and when one's turn is up we will turn back around to see how far the mountain has moved." Shogway agreed to this, and so they turned.

The stranger went first. When he was satisfied that he had moved the mountain, they turned back around. Shogway was surprised to see that the mountain had indeed moved, although only a little bit.

"Now it's my turn", Shogway said, and they turned their backs on the mountain once more. There was a commotion and noise behind them, and, out of curiosity, the stranger turned back around before they had agreed to it. Little did he know that Shogway had moved the mountain so close to the stranger's back that when he turned to look **he struck his face on it.** The force of the impact bent his nose and **left one side of his face crooked**.
At this, the stranger conceded that Shogway was the more powerful of the two, and that he must also be the creator of the land and everything on it.

Shogway then had to decide what to do about the stranger. Because he had moved the mountain (if only a little bit), the stranger indeed was possessed of a certain degree of power, and the Creator thought that it would not do to let such a being remain on the earth; he was about to populate the earth with people, and to let this stranger coexist with them might not be a good thing. He told the stranger so, and proposed that he would have to remove him from the land. The stranger pleaded with Shogway, and said that, if he was allowed to stay, he would help the people.

"This is what I will do," the stranger said. "I have the power to control the wind, and I can protect the people in this way. If ever a strong wind or storm threatens them, I will use my cane and block it from destroying their settlements, and I can lift it and send it over their settlements so that it does not blow through. In addition to this, I have the power to heal sickness. If ever the people are struck down with illness they can call on me, and I will help them to get better. This is how they will do it.

When they need aid of me in this way, **they will create a mask whose face is in my image**, and I will hand-pick the men who will create these masks. The very second that they lay the first strike in creating a mask, that fast will it have my power. When they use the mask, they will prepare a certain kind of corn mush, and burn tobacco. The tobacco will form their words which I will hear, and I will come. They will refer to me as their grandfather, and I will help them as long as the earth remains." Shogway agreed to this, and allowed the stranger to stay on the earth.

The ceremony begins with the telling of the myth about Old Broken Nose, then an invocation to the spirits, the ritual, ending with a feast. During the ritual, the False Face members, wearing Iroquois masks, go through every house in the town looking for those who are diseased and ill. If a sick person is found, a healing ritual is performed using turtle shell rattles and blown ashes from tobacco. The community gathers in the longhouse where the False Faces enter, and healings may be requested. It continues with dancing and ends with a ceremonial ash blowing and a feast. It's performed during the spring, fall, midwinter, and smaller version of the ceremony are performed whenever a sick individual requires it.

The Masks

These Iroquois Masks are considered to be "living" and are "fed" with tobacco. The design of the masks may vary, but most share certain features. They have long black or white horse hair. The eyes are deep-set and accented by metal. The noses are bent and crooked. They are painted red and black.

The Power of the Hunt

The act of "hunting" was a serious endeavor for most of humankind's history. Food is life itself and in a time where starvation was a real threat, the hunt took on greater meaning. Hunting involved danger and risk. Angry ferocious animals can react and the hunter became the hunted. A "good hunter" survives; a "poor hunter" perishes. But it was also spiritual.

Concept of Respect

Native American, indigenous people believed animals had souls. They viewed the hunt as something filled with great power and how they conducted themselves to be quite serious.

Thus, the Innu believe that: a hunter does not kill an animal against its will, but with its consent. Hunters and hunted are alike part of nature. As long as ... [they] follow the customs of their people, as handed down from their forefathers, and they do not offend the animals and their spiritual masters, they will continue to live in peace with each other and with nature Henriksen, *Land Use and Occupancy Among the Naskapi of Davis Inlet* , Unpublished report for the Naskapi Montagnais Innu Association.1977: 8.

These rules of respect include placing the bones of the animals killed on outdoor scaffolds, in trees, or lakes and streams, making sure that the dogs do not eat the bones, placing animal fat and left-overs in the fire, consuming the fat from the caribou long bones, and wearing decorated clothing while hunting Vaino Tanner, *Outlines of the Geography, Life and Customs of Newfoundland-Labrador (the Eastern Part of the Labrador Peninsul)*, Helsinki, Finland, 1944: 643).

Respect is shown to the black bear by referring to it as *Nimushum* (grandfather) or *Nukum* (grandmother), and by ensuring that it is treated in a proper ritualistic manner when it is killed.

Rituals for the hunt have existed for millennia; whether smearing with blood, or dancing for days before the hunt. Perhaps they point to deep understandings of man and animals and man's place in the world.

Modern man has lost some of this connection and a yearning may exist to touch these deeper knowings again. Modern day hunting rituals may include 6-packs of beer and camaraderie. But the mystical lurks barely below the surface.

All Our Relations

Man has a relationship with animals. What kind of relationship is it?

"*Mitakuye oyasin*", the Lakota expression says "all our relations", and points to the interconnectedness of all living creatures.

The act of capture or the kill can be seen as a moment of great power, a sacred exchange of life.

I have encountered wild animals while meditating in the forest. These are moments of great power. The same power is felt by hunters. Ancient man left few writings but we can use historical accounts within the last few hundred years.

Hunt *(dictionary definition)*: to search persistently for something difficult to find

Hunting was a crucial component of hunter-gatherer societies before the domestication of animals. With the establishment of language and culture, hunting became a theme of stories and myths, aphorisms, adages, and metaphors which continue even today. To hunt an animal successfully requires a deep intimate knowledge of its habits and life.

Clans: It may sound strange or quaint to read about the clans in native American tribes: Wolf Clan, Bear Clan, Snake Clan etc. What all this implies is a reverence of animals as intelligent beings, worthy of devotion.

For example, if the Wolf was your "totem", the wolf would bestow its hunting prowess to you, its perseverance in the hunt. The gifts of a wolf are given to you. For that gift, you reciprocate by never hunting or eating the wolf, and by other ceremonial activities of devotion.

It is a duty of the totem to guard the ritualist and the medicine man while he is asleep. In the case of danger or the arrival of strangers, the animal goes back into the body of the medicine man and informs him. After the death of the medicine man, the animal stands watch as a bright flickering light near the grave. The individual totem is also a helper of the medicine man. The medicine man emits the totem in his sleep or in a trance so that it can collect information for him.

Among most tribes and indigenous or ancient peoples there is a perceived need for reciprocity with nature. Humans and animals have obligations to each other and failure to honor those obligations can be dangerous.

Success in hunting and fishing is dependent on the good will of the Great Spirit and the spiritual realm of the animals. Animals are thought to have "animal masters" who must be appeased at the spiritual level, through ceremony and respect.

Animals are believed to have essentially the same sort of animating agency which man possesses. They have a language of their own, can understand what human beings say and do, have forms of tribal or social organization, and live a life which is parallel in other respects to that of human society. Irving Hallowell, *Bear Ceremonialism in the Northern Hemisphere,* American Anthropologist, Jan-Mar 1926 p.7)

Many medicine men state there was a time when man and animals communicated freely and directly with each other In modern days, man is not in tune with this deep link with animals. This former communication allowed the animals to instruct man in man things, in medicine and survival.

The Holy Hunt

Many native people lived in an aware world. Wherever they went, they were amongst spirits of their ancestors, as well as those of the animals, plants, hills, winds, lakes and rivers.

The native people were admonished to never do harm, abuse or even make fun of animals. Since they lived in an aware world, the animals would always know.

A traditional hunter plumbs the depth of his intellect - his capacity to manipulate complex knowledge. But he also delves into his animal nature, drawing from intuitions of sense and body and heart; feeling the wind's touch, listening for the tick of moving ice, peering from crannies, hiding himself as if he were the hunted.

He moves in a world of eyes, where everything watches - the bear, the seal, the wind, the moon and stars, the drifting ice, the silent waters below. He is beholden to powers greater than his own.

Hunting Rituals
Pre-Hunt
Ancient peoples often danced prior to the hunt.

What is Dance?
"Dancing is a language, an articulated language of the body, asserting human individual rhythm in harmony with the rhythms of Nature" Maria Silva Codecasa, "*Of Knots and Dots and Coconuts: Divination in Micronesia*".

Dance was prayer to the native peoples. Dance was a way to honor the animal spirits.

Dance was knowledge. Just as today science recognizes the constant recurrence of simple, tiny atomic particles in all sort of organized matter, our ancestors had the intuition that there was **a secret rhythm in Nature** which was the same in every single natural manifestation. A crane dance must mirror star dances, and human dance is an alphabet to decipher the unknown.

Accounts of Virginia Indian Tribes – Jamestown colony

Powhatan Indians made ritual offerings, or sacrifices, in order to appease Okee, (a great spirit who controlled hunting).

John Smith observed that this was a major responsibility of the *kwiocosuk* or medicine man. But just as ordinary men could commune with spirits as necessary, so they offered minor sacrifices when the occasion required it. At least among the high-ranking members of society, it was common to throw a bit of food into the fire as a thankful offering before eating the main meal of the day.

Similarly, a sacrifice — usually deer's blood or suet on a large stone altar, or *pawcorance*—was required before beginning any important activity or upon one's return from a successful hunt or raid.

First Kill

In First Kill rituals at the first kill of a young hunter, the boy is seen to pass from boyhood to manhood, from feminine influence to the world of the masculine. In a way the hunter represents competition over cooperation, and selfishness over selflessness. It may involve the blood of the animal. Examples: washing in the blood of a deer, smearing the deer blood on one's face.

Ancient German Ritual: There is a German hunting tradition where the hunter places an evergreen twig in the mouth of the game just killed and places one in his hat. The name of the Branch Sign that is placed in the mouth is the "**letzter Bissen**" which literally means "last bite" and is a mark of respect to the game.

The origin of these traditions goes back a long way. "Branch Signs" were included. They are principally a method of signals between hunters to convey a series of important messages and include warnings, directions to follow, routes not to follow and many others.

It is interesting to note that many of the mainland European nations have a similar, and in some cases, identical, form of signs.

Bear Ritual

The bear was powerful to native Americans. One reason is that the bear walked on 2 legs erect, resembling the human.

Because of their size and weight, bears were usually butchered in the field before being transported back to camp. Before the hide was removed, it was ritually shaken three times. The flesh was stripped from the bones, but the entrails were saved. The hide might be used to cover the meat or it might be fashioned into a pouch to carry the meat and fat Da Laguna 1972:366.

Emmons (1991:133) remarked that "The bones of the head and the feet were either buried deep in the ground, or cast into the sea. But withal, its flesh was eaten, and its pelt was used like that of any other animal."

Before being put to general use, the hide itself was treated with great care.

Before preparing the meat for consumption and storage, a short ritual was often conducted which included warming the bear's head and putting the tongue and the heart, smothered in seal grease, on a stick.

As the stick was held over the fire, one or more songs were sung to the bear's head. These songs were learned from the bear people. If this ritual was conducted properly, the bear's spirit would be pleased, and good weather would prevail for drying the skin. If the bear was not treated properly, it would rain continuously, and drying would be difficult. The rain was believed to be "the eyes of the brown bear crying". George Jim, pers. comm. 1990, Thomas F. Thornton, Alaska Department of Fish and Game Technical Paper No. 214, February 1992.

.

Inland Tlingit hunters also usually leave the skins of both black and grizzly bears outside the camp for several days, with the head part pointed towards the sun, and the fur inside out. 'You do this so the bear people think good of it. [think that] you treat it with respect.' McClellan, Catherine, *My Old People Say: An Enthnographic Survey of Southern Yukon Territory*, 1975

Sometimes, 'especially when they are bothered' by bear spirits, hunters put swan's down on the skin and treat it with red paint...Two grizzly skins must never be laid or hung tail to tail because 'you split your luck.'" *Subsistence Use Of Brown Bear In Southeast Alask*a, Thomas F. Thornton, excerpted From Alaska Department of Fish and Game Technical Paper No. 214, February 1992.

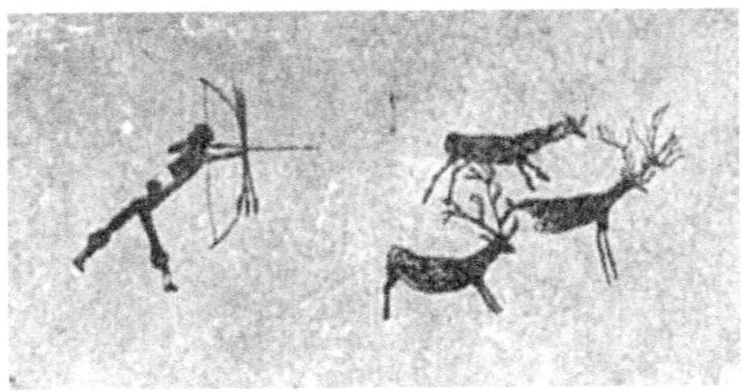

Ancient rituals and rites for hunting indicate man's attempts to understand his animal brethren and this sacred interaction. By studying these ancient ways perhaps man can reconnect with this perspective of viewing animals as more than our food, but as powerful creatures in their own right.

Bigfoot Accounts

Accounts can be traced back to early native traditions and even the logs of explorer Samuel de Champlain describe a tall, ape-like creature that roamed the rugged mountains and forests of northern New York and Vermont.

In his ship's log chronicling his voyage of discovery on the St. Lawrence River 1604, Champlain wrote how numerous Indian tribes in the region had told eerie stories of a giant, hairy man-beast that was known to the natives as "the Gougou".

Champlain wrote that so many of the tribes recounted such stories that he believed there must be some truth to the tales. Several natives told him of their escape, and others of having heard the Gougou's "horrible noises" as they passed by its home.

"What makes me believe what they say," Champlain wrote, "is the fact that all the savages fear it, and tell such strange things about it." Certainly, we cannot accuse these early natives of being "publicity hounds" promoting hoaxes, as they had no obvious motives to fabricate bigfoot accounts.

The Iroquois have a similar oral history of flesh-eating stone giants who possessed powerful physiques. In Quebec, the Algonquins called these creatures "Kokotshe".

In northern Vermont, Abenaki traditions tell of a huge, hairy, man-like creature known as the Forest Wanderer who would leave giant, human-like footprints behind. In the 18th and early 19th centuries, many early Vermont settlers told of encountering a mysterious bear that moved swiftly through the woods on two legs, always managing to elude capture.

In the 1700s, colonial frontiersman Robert Rogers and his Rangers were pursued by something in the north woods. One of Roger's Rangers claimed the creature had legs as large as spruce logs.

Other accounts:
Jose Mariano Mocino was a naturalist from New Spain and in 1792 he was part of an exploration and scientific expedition to British Columbia. He wrote an account of his travels in *Noticias de Nutka: An Account of Nootka Sound* in 1792. He noted in his book on exploration that the native people of the Pacific Northwest feared a creature who lived in the woods. They referred to it as "Matlox"

Jose wrote: "I do not know what to say about Matlox, inhabitant of the mountainous district, of who all have an unbelievable terror. They imagine his body as very monstrous, all covered with stiff black bristles; a head similar to a human one, but with much greater, sharper, and stronger fangs than those of the bear; extremely long arms; and toes and fingers armed with long curved claws. His shouts alone (they say) force those who hear them to the ground, and any unfortunate body he slaps is broken into a thousand pieces."

José didn't witness the creatures personally.

The Nootka Indians also used a variation of "Matlose".

There are Eskimo accounts gathered from early 1800s Russian explorers, and stories gathered from Southern California's mission Indians by Spanish priests in the late 1700s. *"Bigfoot/Sasquatch Resurgence of Native American Indian Legends"*

Is the Sasquatch more than just physical? Many tribes believed it is an inter-dimensional being which appears to help his human brothers during crisis. Eyewitness accounts state that one of the characteristics of some Sasquatch is the ability to suddenly appear or disappear. This belief may explain why his physical remains are not located.

Bigfoot and Missionary Accounts

Elkanah Walker was a missionary to the Spokane Indians of Northern Washington. The following is a letter he addressed to Reverend David Green, the secretary of the American Board of Commissioners for Foreign Missions.

Elkanah Walker in April of 1840 wrote:
..."I suppose you will bear with me if I trouble you with a little of their superstition, which has recently come to my

knowledge. They believe in the existence of a race of giants which inhabit a certain mountain off to the west of us. This mountain is covered with perpetual snow. They inhabit its top. They may be classed with Goldsmith's nocturnal class and they cannot see in the daytime. They hunt and do all of their work in the night...

They come to the people's lodges in the night when the people are asleep and take them, and put them under their skins and take them to their place of abode without even waking. When they wake in the morning they are wholly lost, not knowing in what direction their home is. The account that they give of these Giants will in some measure correspond with the Bible account of this race of beings. ..They say their track is about a foot and a half long. They will carry two or three beams upon their back at once. They frequently come in the night and steal their salmon from their nets and eat the'm raw. If the people are awake they always know when they are coming very near, by their strong smell, which is most intolerable. It is not uncommon for them to come in the night and give three whistles and then the stones will begin to hit their houses. The people believe that they are still troubled with their nocturnal visits. We need the prayers of the Church at home.

Rain-Making

There are numerous accounts of medicine men making rain during droughts. Rainmaking is a weather modification ritual that attempts to invoke rain.

***Rainmaking among the Mandan*, George Catlin, 1837**

North American rain dances were performed by many Native American tribes, particularly in the South West area of the country. A Native American rain dance is unlike other dances. It's more complicated. It's not just a circle; it's a pattern woven over and over again. And the dances could go on for hours.

It is believed that the Native Americans often tracked and followed known weather patterns, and also offered to perform rain dances for settlers in return for trade items. In particular, the feathered masked rain dance of the Zuni people of New Mexico has been well documented.

The ancient art of rainmaking was once practiced all around the world. It represented the sacred relationship between humans and the Divine and a subtle understanding of energy.

The art of rainmaking is still practiced today in a few places in Africa, Australia, New Zealand, and wherever some knowledge of the old way remains.

A recent interesting documentary film "*Putuparri and the Rainmakers*" follows an aboriginal shaman who makes rain in the driest part of Australia. Watch film Trailer here: https://youtu.be/df1oBqabHBw

Some medicine men created rain by first creating "ritual rain." The simplest method was to throw water into the air, as did the Pomo, Coast Miwok, and Yokuts.

"Interestingly, the control of rain was believed to be related to the tribal affiliation of the rain shaman. To illustrate, a Kawaiisu rain shaman did not have the power to stop rain that had been produced by a Tübatulabal or Yokuts colleague". Jerry N. Hopkins et. al. *Further Reflections on California Rain-Making Shamanism: " The Other Half " of the Tübatulabal Shaman's Rain-Making Bundle*

Here is an article from 1998 at CNN News concerning a rain dance performed in Brazil to end a drought.

INDIGENOUS WM - SOUTH AMERICA

Strong rains fall on fire-ravaged Amazon stateá
March 31, 1998á
Web posted at: 6:46 p.m. EST (2346 GMT)á

BRASILIA, Brazil (CNN) -- The first strong rains in six months fell Tuesday on the remote Amazon state of Roraima, kindling hopes that wildfires that have raged out of control for three months would soon end.á
The rains fell on dried forests one day after two Caiapo Indian shamans were flown to the Yanomami reservation to perform a special ritual they believed would bring rain.

"If it's a coincidence or not, I don't know, but it certainly seemed to have done the trick," said Alan Suassuna, press spokesman for the Federal Indian Bureau in Boa Vista, the Roraima state capital located 1,550 miles northwest of Brasilia.

The ritual performed Monday night involved dancing, praying and the gathering of leaves, Suassuna said. Heavy rains started at about 9:30 a.m. and lasted about four hours, he said. Suassuna estimated the rains quenched 80 percent to 90 percent of the fires but said an accurate evaluation will not be possible until Wednesday, when the army has flown over the area.

Newly available satellite photos show that about 13,200 square miles -- about 15 percent of the state -- have been devastated by the fires, which were set by subsistence farmers

Florida – Seminole Medicine Man:

In 1985, a Seminole medicine man was requested to make rain in the Tampa, Florida region during an intense drought which plagued the area. Here is an account (Seminole Tribune, Peter Gallagher, 2/22/2012):

"When Seminole medicine man Bobby Henry has to make it rain, he tosses a live gopher tortoise into the air. That angers the gods because 'turtles not s'posed to fly,' he said. When the gods get sufficiently angry, they roar with thunder and hurl spears of lighting. If Bobby keeps throwing that turtle up, or if he adds a frog, as he did when he ended the drought in Tampa several years ago, the furious gods will send down torrents of angry rain.

But there is obviously more to it than that. You and I can throw reptiles or amphibians into the air and nothing would happen.

There are ancient words that Bobby utters in his native language and thoughts in his mind that no one can know about, he said. Some of this came to him naturally not long after he was born, in the mid-1930s, out in the cypress swamps near Ochopee on the Tamiami Trail. He doesn't know why, and he doesn't really want to talk a lot about it. In traditional enigmatic fashion, however, he will give you his commercial business card. It reads "Rainmaker" and lets you know how to reach him if you need a canoe, a totem pole or a chickee hut built.

Or if you need it to rain.

Bobby is personable, always mixing humor and humility with a smile and a handshake for all. He turned 75 last month. Bobby Henry is powerful and very respected by all Indians. Bobby is the most famous medicine man in the world."

As a little boy, he said he was taken aside and provided special training. What to eat and how to cure.

"***Hear the owl, respect panther, stare with snake's eye***," is all he will say.

Once, during a severe 1985 drought in West Central Florida, Bobby was summoned to the steps of City Hall; exasperated municipal officials were worried about the area's dwindling water supply and out-of-control fires.

With newspapers and television stations documenting the event and former Tampa Mayor Bob Martinez looking on, Bobby got out the turtle and the frog. Immediately following his ceremony, the skies mysteriously darkened, and rain fell in torrents. Area weathermen, who were predicting no end to the drought in sight, were shocked. The Associated Press sent word of the miracle around the world. The Rainmaker was born.

Another time, severe rain threatened a scheduled Pow-Wow. Thunder could be heard in the distance. As one of the DNA event producers, I saw months of hard work about to be drowned. Suddenly, through the fog, Bobby walked by. “Bobby,” I implored, “can’t you make it not rain?”

He suddenly pulled a gigantic knife from a scabbard handing on his side. “Sure,” he said. “Cut the clouds.”

He walked off by himself, holding the knife high and still, as if slicing the atmosphere as he strolled. For a good hour, he walked back and forth the length of that football field, through that smoky fog, saying words no one could understand, thinking thoughts no one will ever know, holding his knife high. Indians from all over North America, in traditional Tribal garb, stood silently on the sidelines watching him in awe.

Suddenly, the sun peeked and then came gloriously out. A great cheering commenced among all present. Even the weatherman on TV was amazed the storm passed Jacksonville by in such a manner. Swelled with rainwater, the black thunderhead traveled more than 100 miles west, where it finally stalled and dumped the predicted deluge right atop the other pow-wow.

I was there. I saw it. It's true.

I went to shake his hand. The fog was gone. He saw me running across the field. "Bobby Henry!" he yelled his own name out to me, his ruddy face all twinkling and smiling; the gods having come through for him once again.

"Bobby Henry! Good medicine!"

"See, here's where you screwed up."

~~~~~~~~~~~~~~~~~~~~~~~~~~~~
~~~~~~~~~~~~~~~~~~~~~~~~~~~~

Conclusion

Native Indian populations were ravaged by diseases brought by the Europeans such as smallpox. "The Great Dying" in New England in the 1600s, is thought to have claimed the lives of 75-90% of the native population – with reports that in several places all the former inhabitants had died. The psychological trauma of survivors ran deep.

Some native people lost faith in their traditional spiritual practices and the medicine men who could not save them from the epidemics.

And yet one cannot ignore the numerous accounts of their supernatural powers. Credible witnesses such as Jesuit priests, although disdaining their practices, related mysterious events and abilities they had witnessed.

Many native people still believe. We must give some credence to practices used for thousands of years. If we suspend disbelief and listen with an open mind and heart, we may sense a deep and mysterious world. A world were animals talk and man recalls his connection to the great mystery.

It is said we all have healing power. One cannot separate the healer from the plant, from the patient. They are all part of one beautiful energetic matrix.

In remote areas, far from prying eyes, the tribes have continued to practice ancient ceremonies. **The power endures.**

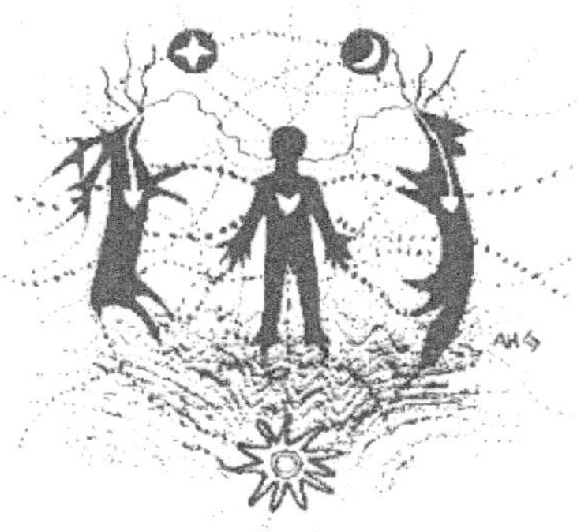

HEALING SONG

NOW all my singing Dreams are gone,
But none knows where they have fled
Nor by what trails they have left me.

Return, O Dreams of my heart,
And sing in the Summer twilight,
By the creek and the almond thicket
And the field that is bordered with lupins!

Now is my refuge to seek
In the hollow of friendly shoulders,
Since the singing is stopped in my pulse
And the earth and the sky refuse me;
Now must I hold by the eyes of a friend
When the high white stars are unfriendly.

Over-sweet is the refuge for trusting;
Return and sing, O my Dreams,
In the dewy and palpitant pastures,
Till the love of living awakes
And the strength of the hills to uphold me.
From the Paiute.

Contact author by email: safeinthewoods@gmail.com

This material is informational only – it is not intended to replace medical diagnosis. Great care must be made when picking wild plants – some plants are very poisonous . ** Use caution*

Printed in Great Britain
by Amazon

62637779R00068